THE PHOTOGRAPHER

Poetry Introduction 4
(with Cal Clothier, Anne Cluysenaar, Alistair Elliot,
Alan Hollinghurst and Craig Raine)
The Slant Door
November and May
Short Wave

GEORGE SZIRTES

The Photographer
in Winter

*To Derek — with many
thanks for his kind
hospitality —*

George Szirtes 86

SECKER & WARBURG
LONDON

First published in England 1986 by
Martin Secker & Warburg Limited
54 Poland Street, WIV 3DF

British Library Cataloguing in Publication Data

Szirtes, George

The photographer in winter.
I. Title
821.914   PR6069.Z/

ISBN 0–436–50995–4

Typeset by Inforum Ltd, Portsmouth
Printed in Great Britain by
Redwood Burn Ltd, Trowbridge

*For my father and mother and those who
live in the courtyards*

ACKNOWLEDGEMENTS

Acknowledgements are due to *Argo, Encounter, Helix, The Honest Ulsterman, The Listener, The Literary Review, The New Hungarian Quarterly, The Observer, Outposts, The Pen, Poetry Australia, The Poetry Book Society Supplement, Poetry Review, The Rialto, The Times Literary Supplement,* where many of these poems first appeared.

'Windows, Shadows' appeared in *Between Comets,* an anthology of poems published for Norman Nicholson's seventieth birthday.

'The Green Mare's Advice to the Cows' was commissioned by the Tate Gallery.

'The Courtyards', 'The Swimmers' and 'The Photographer in Winter' were broadcast by the BBC in a programme entitled *Water, Snow and Ice.* 'Changing Names' and 'The Child I Never Was' were broadcast on BBC3's *Poetry Now.*

Chief acknowledgements though are due to the Arts Council of Great Britain, whose bursary enabled me to revisit Hungary in 1984, for the first time since leaving it in 1956. Without their generosity this book could not have been written.

CONTENTS

THE PHOTOGRAPHER IN WINTER

(i.m. M.S. 1924–1975)
for M.V. and O.O.

'He was hurrying along with frozen hands and watering eyes when he saw her not ten metres away from him. It struck him at once that she had changed in some ill-defined way.' – Orwell

It must have been an office.
He must have spoken to you quietly,
the snow a softening presence through the window.
His voice was snow, white twists of powder
with consonants of ice, a draught of vowels:
This is the way we work. We look and listen.

It must have been like that. But I can see you
waiting for the end of the year's snow,
the whispering room grown white as a dead face
that wants to make a noise but falls to flakes.
The whole era has been sealed in ice:
You must be reasonable. Look and listen.

You must simply go on saying No.
No-one can touch you now or ever again.
It's snowing in the crematorium
where you are named, the pond is frozen,
but under it the offices are open:
We don't ask much. It's such a simple matter.

*

You touch your skin. Still young. The wind blows waves
of silence down the street. The traffic grows
a hood of piled snow. The city glows.
The bridges march across a frozen river
which seems to have been stuck like that for ever.
The elderly keep slipping into graves.

Your camera is waiting in its case.
What seems and is has never been less certain –
the room is fine, but there beyond the curtain
the world can alter shape. You watch and listen.
The mirror in the corner seems to glisten
with the image of a crystalline white face.

Too many marvels. Pagodas, ziggurats;
the follies of the snow. Geometries
in miniature, the larger symmetries
of cars, the onion domes of bollards, spires
on humble kiosks, stalactites on wires,
a vast variety of dazzling hats.

The white face in the mirror mists and moves
obscure as ever. Waves of silence roll
across the window. You are in control
of one illusion as you close your eyes.
The room, at least, won't take you by surprise
and even in the dark you find your gloves.

*

Where are you going? To work? I'm watching you.
You cannot get away. I have been trained
To notice things. But all will be explained
And you will know why it is necessary
To follow you like this. In the meantime, carry
On as usual, do what you would normally do.

You catch the tram? I'll sit behind you where
You will not find me. I see your every move.
Believe me when I say you would approve
Such thoroughness and objectivity.
So this is the route you take across the city.
The tram goes rattling on. You touch your hair

Before you stand and walk off down the street.
Your hair is swinging loosely. The snow breaks
My picture up. It needs a few more takes
To get this right. Your costume is correct
Historically speaking? They will expect
Immaculate appearances, discreet

Camera angles, convincing details. Please
Co-operate with me and turn your head,
Smile vacantly as if you were not dead
But walked through parallel worlds. Now look at me
As though you really meant it. I think we could be
Good for each other. Hold it right there. Freeze.

*

You can't remember and you can't redeem
the faces altered with a loaded brush,
faces who drift before you as you wash
the prints in faint red light, pure images
of births and funerals and marriages.
The snow has lost them. Even when you dream

they merge confusingly. The children throw
white bombs at one another which explode
splattering their clothes; and, across the road,
a white-haired man reveals his youthful skin.
You see the building he's been living in
and you yourself have aged. He turns to go

but leaves his face behind, a different face
with no expression but the features set.
You cannot quite remember where you met
but go on meeting. Doorways, offices.
The dream creates an odd paralysis.
He seems to move, you're frozen in your place.

Wake up, wake up. The faces disappear.
Your own must be put on. You look a mess
and draw a veil over your tiredness.
The curtains lift. Your hair must be swept back
before the wind which gives you a loud smack
and forces out an unexploded tear.

*

Some elegance is what you crave, a touch
of silver in the grey light of the street,
a hint of Strauss to fill the room, the beat
of the Radetzky March, or other such
imperial themes. Ironic music, gay,
but not unfitting in its own small way.

Exaggerations, nothing more. You climb
eight flights of stairs, immerse yourself
in private smells. The novels on the shelf
begin to yellow. You can measure time
in their coarse pages, in the damp, the space
between the deadpan mirror and your face.

The mirror throws her silvered answer back.
A breath takes you away beyond the glass
into a land of fog and rain. Hours pass
like dim processions, tiny boats, a track
of dirty water, and the music plays
while breath evaporates. The image stays.

The gods of gracious living pass us by.
They hear you vaguely as the marches fade
above the humming of their motorcade.
Dear woman, train your photographic eye
on me and the dead wall where I must wait
for you to reappear, however late.

*

Hand colouring. It was a form of art,
And when you bent over your work I saw
How art could not obey a natural law,
That faces flowered and that teeth shone pale
As distant neon: memory would fail
To keep the living and the dead apart.

To be quite honest, it was creepy watching
This process of embalmment (as it seemed),
To see the smoothed-out features, the redeemed
Perfection of the unbelievable, showing
No signs of ever having lived, but glowing
Pink and white. I found it strangely touching.

And that was art, you said. The difficult.
But you were lying or just didn't know,
And even then, so many years ago,
The images had started to assume
The frozen aspect of an empty room,
Imperfect, white and granular as salt.

And now it's winter, and this dreadful weather
Is always at the very edge of spring
But cannot make or fake it. I can't bring
Another year to light. You sit alone
With all the pictures that the wind has blown
Away and art must somehow fit together.

*

This winter is not metaphorical.
The sun has broken into tiny pieces
And goes on fracturing as it releases
More and more light, which decorates the walls
With stud-medallions and hangs up crystals
On high wires, where they shudder, trip and fall

And break again. Sometimes it is water
Creeping down a window, a sharpened pen
Above the lintel, a white screen which men
Must penetrate like knives, a curious shriek
Which cuts the eye. A square of film must seek
To capture intact this wild and wholesale slaughter.

I go on taking pictures all the same.
I shoot whole rolls of film as they shoot me.
We go on clicking at the world we see
Disintegrating at our fingers' ends,
As if, by stopping time, we made amends
For all that time destroyed outside the frame.

I watch her working. Now and then I've tried
To catch her eye but found the snow had grown
A brilliance which sunlight made its own
And broke on impulse, as it breaks a train
Of thought, or breaks (it seems) a windowpane
That seems to show her on the other side.

*

What awful cold we seem to have had this year.
A winter of betrayals. Even words
Drop dead in flight, and, afterwards,
We try to sweep them up, quite uselessly.
I can hardly see a hand in front of me.
Everything is speckled. Nothing is clear.

Imagine trying to focus through this swirl
And cascade of snow. It's dark already.
Impossible to keep the picture steady
In the wind. An early evening filters in
Behind the white – my gloves are much too thin
To keep it out. I think I am a girl.

'To be alone in winter is like dying,'
She sings. Here everyone is alone. We die
Of the cold. It can be dangerous to cry
When tears freeze on your cheeks. We must have courage
And think of winter as a happy marriage,
The kiss of snow, the wind's contented sighing.

We must have courage till the spring regains
Her confidence. Courage is everything.
I load the camera and slowly bring
The landscape into focus. My heart stutters
But my hand is firm, and as I click the shutter
I feel the cold blood thawing in my veins.

*

I see you standing there, not quite full length.
Successive sheets of ice preserve and bear
You up, first as a girl with wavy hair,
And then a prisoner, a skeleton
Just gathering new flesh. The layers go on
So fast that I am troubled by your strength.

But fainter now, you're sitting in a chair
And wasting away under a fall of snow.
Once more under the skin the faint bones show
Their X-rays. The fragility of ice
Is starting to break up and once or twice
The water spreads across you like fine hair,

Fine hair confusing everything, now dark,
Now light, whichever way the double vision
Catches it. I'm angling for position,
Betraying you with your own camera.
The winter offers vague ephemera
And leaves behind no trace or watermark.

There's nothing to betray. I am exposed
And doubled. I have grown two faced, split skins,
Become a multiple. Something begins
To bother me – I think it's my own voice.
The situation offers me no choice –
The shutter's open. Now the shutter's closed.

THE BUTTON MAKER'S TALE

Once I had a shop where I made buttons,
but buttons sank like lead, without a trace.
I lost my money and I lost my buttons,
but I was young and didn't give a fig.

The next time I put money into figs,
but figs were almost unobtainable.
I lost my money and I lost my figs.
The whole affair was most embarrassing.

After that I couldn't do much better
than put my money into foreign postcards.
(Saucy postcards! Who'll buy saucy postcards?)
The moral climate changed within a year.

I can't help it. I have this sort of hunger
for risk and failure. So I took up hunger,
which wasn't then a scarce commodity –
people bought it and paid me with their curses.

So last I put my money into damns.
The time was ripe and all the tills were ringing,
my little chicks were coming home to roost.
But my lot was with damns and not with chickens.

I was waiting for the Revolution,
but when it came it caught us unprepared.
We lost our money (some of us lost lives)
and ceased to trade at all, except in jokes,

of which this story is a specimen.
You'll not deny it has a certain length
generous for the times, and, much like buttons,
serves to hold these tattered clothes together.

THE SWIMMERS

Inside the church the floor is like black ice:
The past moves underneath it as it glimmers
In the light of the long windows, and you read
In brass the images of the dead swimmers.

Shoal on shoal, the fluidity of bodies
Supports the weight of the whole edifice.
The names, resemblances and epithets
Run by beneath your feet, under the ice.

Nowhere more than in churches are you aware
Of treading water. Surely you must sink
Under the weight of your own body: the building
Itself becomes nebulous and starts to shrink,

But the swimming goes on undisturbed. The dead
Press water and each other down the centuries
Of darkness: dear small girls, their sisters, mothers,
Husbands, families, their towns, whole countries

Float in the river which runs steadily
Dissolving everything. No wonder
The churches smell of damp and sadness.
The present drips from walls, the rest go under.

*

Like Venables Hinde, infant of the parish,
Along with John, Martha and Bess, of whom
None lived beyond thirty, though each lived longer
Than seven infant Hindes in the same tomb.

History is prodigal with numbers
And Venables Hinde was simply singular:
I think of him now drifting in his coffin,
Properly snuffed, tucked and rectangular,

With solemn messages about him; warnings,
Talismans, to *Remember Eternity*,
Or else to *Redeem Time*, or a plain *Here Lieth*.
For truisms we have immense capacity

And Venables had not yet grown out of them,
A small round passive cliché, hardly elliptical,
His utterances flat and loud, mere noise
Between one or other mortal receptacle.

Poor swimmers, hardly strength enough to move
And yet constrained to buttress a whole chapel.
Tread lightly here, respect the concentration
Of these verbose and delicate people.

*

Who's lost, who's found? I've looked here for you sometimes
And tried to feel such correspondences
As time redeems, remembering . . . I've strained
To hear you speak coherent sentences,

Cloud-cuckoo tongues, High Dutch or a pure Greek,
A tongue as washed out and as disinfected
As the water; full of hesitations
And precise declensions, but quite unaffected.

How foreign they all sound. How far downstream
From the familiar parish. Their formal prose
Has stiffened into marble but the tongues
Wag on, like plants, in a tide that comes and goes . . .

Drowned hands and skin; the water drifting off
Becoming water. Their bodies are unknown
As are the names you lived by. Who'll lay claim
To this faint draft of skin, this line of bone?

Whose element is water? A vacuous bright room
Waits upstairs. You approach it quietly –
Like rising through the sea and hearing nothing –
No names, no objects, no singing, nothing but sea.

*

Some forty years ago a girl was drowning
In the icy Danube, one of a great number
Shot that day in the last week of the Terror.
Time and again she seemed to have gone under,

But rose once more, raising a stiff arm.
Between the floes she drifted perilously.
As Hemingway said, Some die hard like cats,
And a cat was what she was most obviously.

But cats as swimmers? Yes, a miracle,
Her jaw shot half away, how she pressed forward.
The Danube was as dullish red as she:
That single arm conveyed the creature shoreward.

Those who remained below grew slippery
And featureless. Unfortunate the disparity
Between high-fliers and the deeply drowned.
She had something of an angel's clarity.

I hear that splashing as they throw her in,
The ripples spreading grey and red and white
From the small body, echoing in the stone.
The hymns begin. The cats sing in the night.

NOTES OF A SUBMARINER

There's not a single window on the craft.
Each bunk is curtained off in tiers of black.
All day you pass along the narrow shaft:
all night you try to jump the passage back.

A form of claustrophobia; the dream
is much repeated and becomes a bore.
You're buried alive but no one hears the scream.
The lid comes down as someone shuts the door.

Then dreams again. You dream in chorus now,
some hundred bodies, separately interred,
gesticulating, one unholy row.
Then order once more, the official word.

No terminus in sight, the night sways on
and burrows deeply. The propellers turn
on unseen wonders that have come and gone,
Edwardian splendours of the age of Verne.

Such harmony of words informs the sea
and regulates the opening hours of clams.
Our lives are disciplined elaborately
into procedures, charts and pentagrams.

Returning to Jules Verne, I thought I saw
the ghost of old Professor Arronax,
his mouth stretched wide in one great gasp of awe,
drifting by beyond the curtain tracks.

We shoulder aside the waves and scoop the deeper
infrastructures of the vegetation,
its outlandish architecture, while the sleeper
nuzzles forward towards the nightmare station.

The voyage is phantasmal, no mistake,
adhering to a magical routine.
A paper girl bends so far back she breaks
across the pages of a magazine.

Old Arronax, Ned Land, the inky squid,
observe the progress of our nautilus
with sinkings of the heart. Our dreams will bid
to settle our accounts and weep for us.

THE COURTYARDS

1

As if a mind subsumed its intellect,
an ear tuned in to noise within the skull,
a mouth spoke words of greeting to a dull
audience of teeth, or an eye observed
the rigging of its fibres and the curved
elastic walls where images collect;

as if a street had turned its stately back
on public matters, and had found a way
of contemplating its own poverty,
had rattled up its years of emptiness
and counted them out on an abacus
of winding stairs, or on a curtain track;

the small lift shuts and forces itself up
a narrow throated shaft with groans of chains
and pulleys, and the whole building complains;
but as you rise through slices of pale light
the brown intensifies to cream, and white,
a trancelike ring of silence at the top.

2

Think of a glove turned neatly inside out;
think of your hand running along a rail
as children run down galleries grown stale
with refuse; think of hands reversed; of keys
and locks; think of these blocks as hollow trees
still echoing to something inchoate;

think of fear, precise as a clean hand
searching in dark corners, with the skill
that years of practice manage to instil;
think of locks where keys will never turn;
of rooms where it takes experts to discern
a movement that the eye can't understand:

The inchoate is what gets lost. You hear
a crazy woman singing, . . . *Tannenbaum,
O tannenbaum* . . . but then her words become
confused with curses, shouts of *God* and *Fate*,
and this is not exactly inchoate
but in such imprecision there is fear.

3

Outside, a rusticated, vermiform
ebullience; outside, a cluttering
of pediments, pilasters, pargeting,
embroidery; outside, the balconies
expand in their baroque epiphanies,
their splendid Biedermeyer uniforms;

outside, the casement windows under rolls
of stonework, rough or smooth or both; façades
with manners courtly as old playing cards;
outside, the straining figures stiffly bent
to hold up yet another pediment
disfigured by a web of bulletholes;

outside, the falling masonry, the hard
emphatic counter-patterns of collapse,
the shattered panes and almost hingeless flaps
that bang like toy guns to disturb the dust.
Inside, the iron-work, the lines of rust;
inside, the piles of rubble in the yard.

4

Inside, the caretaker; his wife; his cat;
a cage for small bikes; rows of potted plants
reaching for light; stuff that no one wants
left in the stairwell; little dingy signs
for manicurists, tailors; heavy lines
of washing stretched out tight from flat to flat;

inside, a sort of life. At one o'clock
the ringing feet of children up the stair,
the scrape of chalk where someone scrawls a bare
diagrammatic girl with breasts like bells
and leaves a message in rough capitals;
inside, the noisy opening of locks.

Inside, I think of someone else, a blind
and aged woman treading the fourth floor
as if it were a jetty from a shore
suspended in a band of warming light.
She feels her way to the door opposite.
The hollow building trembles in her hand.

5

Think of an empty room with broken chairs,
a woman praying, someone looking out
and listening for someone else's shout
of vigilance; then think of a white face
covered with fine powder, bright as glass,
intently looking up the blinding stairs.

There's someone moving on a balcony;
there's someone running down a corridor;
there's someone falling, falling through a door,
and someone firmly tugging at the blinds.
Now think of a small child whom no one minds
intent on his own piece of anarchy:

Think of a bottle lobbing through the air
describing a tight arc – one curious puff –
then someone running, but not fast enough.
There's always someone to consider, one
you have not thought of, one who lies alone,
or hangs, debagged, in one more public square.

6

As if the light had quietly withdrawn
into a state of grace; as if the sun
had moved out to the country, or had gone
abroad; as if the shadows had grown old
and grey, or found their recesses too cold
and spread themselves across a civic lawn.

Then what is left? I see the woman grip
the handrail as she feels her way along.
She clutches fervently a ball of string,
an old steel key. She turns the corner, calls
to someone downstairs; and the steel key falls,
suspended like an odd metallic drip.

As if the past could ever lose its teeth:
As if the eye could swallow everything
and leave the world in darkness, blundering
about the courtyards! As if all the words
not spoken here could congregate like birds
and block out the faint noises from beneath!

7

Uncertainly she calls out from the top
of the thin stairs. The key won't fit the lock.
The key won't turn. The key is firmly stuck
inside the door. Then how to get up there
but run up every storey by the stair,
and hope she'll still be there when the stairs stop,

and hope she'll still be there when the stairs stop.

TRAINS:

LEVEL CROSSING

Hearing the transmission of the rain,
   the ticking of static and the insect lectures,
and seeing those corroded pictures
   flaking across the screen beyond the pane,
merely the sound of water on the sill,
   you reassemble time and hold it still.

It makes a pattern that is audible:
   you hear the history of voices, continuous
as traffic, concealing some ingenious
   device for transmuting the bored, trivial
natter of your days. How could you guess
   those intricacies lodged in pettiness?

Re-entering that noise is much like waiting
   for a train. You're at a level crossing,
hearing at first the usual nothings
   of the wind and birds, then a faint curious shaking,
a tickling in the spine, a purr and spring
   before the final awesome clattering.

A lit train, carriages of light. Its going
   is so cheerful. There's no turning back,
only the vague murmuring of the track
   whose love will leave us perfect in our knowing,
to stand in showers, breed memories like rain.
   The stations sing and then it's quiet again.

NORTH CHINA

A man is walking, or appears to walk,
Rapidly backwards into the lit town
Beyond the darkening platform, where a crust
Of light encases him in the dust
Of his own translucence, his head a stalk
Beside our furious clatter.
    These things will cease to matter.

A stutter of pale boards, the names of sleep:
How soon the semiology of shape
And dying fall takes over. Neither past
Nor future, we discover here a lost
Continent of moments, whose elegy
Begins with a drowsy numbness.
    Such continents are nameless.

A city in the extreme north of China
Freezes each year to fifty below zero.
It has an enormous Culture Park where snow
Becomes a polished lawn and festivals
Of sculpture feature houses with ice walls
Embedding bits of china
    Crowned with ice antennae.

Such baroque, such opulence, such darkness.
We're on the edge of all that's frozen, formal,
Furious and unattainable.
The great fantastic trains, like twists of barley,
Go nosing forward rather eerily.
Even a good marriage
    Is more than half a mirage.

GHOST TRAIN

Is it an illusion? It must be. Cesare
Pavese, sitting on a train, in a third-class
Carriage, alone with a woman who smokes.
He is too embarrassed to smile or make a pass
Among those empty seats that other women
Have at times vacated. It is history,
And the long train croaks
And shudders, smelling of upholstery,
Remaining empty, no place for encounters.

Public transport has been stitching together
The unfinished business of old Europe.
Believing in ghost buses that fail to stop
When requested, that appear only in foul weather,
Inhabitants of inner cities glamorise
Familiar places where the traffic chunters
Like some vigilant but dull
Official, an Argus with myopic eyes
Who cannot watch over his human cattle.
The ghost buses are empty, driverless.
They come upon one suddenly, with a noise
Of thunder and faint bells, their progress
Unsteady, vast overgrown toys
That have run away, and found this special route,
These special streets. Now someone tells a story
Of those who have managed the trick of boarding
By somehow leaping on, getting a foot
On the platform and grasping the ghost bar. According
To him their fate is terrible, a gory
Compound of brown wire, a cross between
A prison and a farmyard, shitty, poisonous.

Such buses and such trains keep rolling on.
Infected landscapes watch them, half asleep
And, perversely amorous,
They listen for flirtations in the spin
Of the wheel or the hiss of the smoke.
Now Cesare Pavese will not keep
Appointments, nor at this time of night
Is it possible to stay awake
And see the stations sweeping out of sight.

WINDOWS, SHADOWS

A single carriage whose quartet of ghosts
dies in faint echoes to both left and right;
    mirrors and windows
where one man's letter moves in darker light
he may not read by, and a third man boasts
    a clutch of shadows.

We rush across the landscape like a fake
legation. Can we speak with the same voice
    despite the windows?
Exclusive as they are they leave a choice
between perfections, though it's a mistake
    to count on shadows.

It's freezing here. Beyond is a whole range,
a gallery of portraits that belong
    only to windows.
Yet something on this side will faintly long
to shadow letters, faces, and exchange
    a life for shadows.

No companion could be more attached.
No brother show a greater sympathy
    than these black windows
making fiction out of fiction, and a body
out of nothing. Some windows may be touched
    only by shadows.

THE GREEN MARE'S ADVICE TO THE COWS

i.m. Marc Chagall d.1985

'It seemed that the cow was conducting world politics at that time'
– Marc Chagall

1

What matters is the price of the mare.
What matters is the colour of the street.
What matters is that streets have no colour to speak of
Until we give them colours. The same with names.
What matters is the sound of arguments
And not their content. Arguments are blue,
Which, incidentally, is the colour of the street
(And hence, you see, I show them arguing).
What matters is the Love of God
And never mind if God does not exist.
You make him yellow, just as Christ is white,
But that damn cockerel keeps getting in,
And cows with their seductive eyes and udders,
And violinists who can only scrape.
It is another music altogether
That we dance to – and it isn't much
But it will do, believe me, it will do.

2

Surrender to mere *brio*? Stiff
Heads float off in disbelief
And fingers multiply in grief.

A clock strikes midnight in the air
In homage to Apollinaire.
Let Malevich adore the square.

Those who are less innocent
Castrate, carve up, dissect, invent
With a much sharper instrument.

A brush is fine. In mute arrest
A country bumpkin cups the breast
Of tender Vacha. Cows are best.

Cows will run the government.
Cows have a delightful scent.
Cows produce their Testament.

You watch the carnival proceed
Down muddy streets. The cows will lead
The moujiks home while altars bleed

With gentle bovine sacrifice,
Both melancholy and precise.
You cannot kill the same cow twice.

You see the calf, you see the child
Within the womb: Vitebsk, a wild
Impatience, dirty, undefiled.

The commissars may rave and row,
The housepainters obey you now
And hang the banner of the Cow.

The frozen cow hangs like a star,
And you yourself a commissar –
You start to moo. Yes, you'll go far.

Remember Grandfather, who stood
Before you with his feet in blood:
'Now look here, cow, we must have food.'

First grub, then dreams. But Lenin stands
All topsy-turvy on his hands.
What sacrifice the state demands.

The cows will take you at your word,
Advancing on you in a herd.
One cow takes wing, soars like a bird.

But look up there. The dream clouds fly
Above nightmare artillery
And cows are raining from the sky,

Dead cows, contented cows. It pays
To trust their unaffected ways
And leave their ghosts a land to graze.

3

The Man who is a Cello and the Fish who plays
The Violin are suddenly struck dumb.
The Goat in the Sky grows horns of logic. He weighs
Too much and every puzzle and conundrum
Begins to feel the lack of a solution.
The puritans claim back their revolution.

The poet, no longer cut in pieces, does not lie
Flat on the grass in the formal posture of death.
The egotistic lovers neither kiss nor fly.
The riddled milkmaid sinks down out of breath.
The dead man's candles cannot light the street
And broken bodies rest on tired feet.

The village processions reverse their steps. They realise
The city they inhabit has always been there, waiting.
The samovar slips off the crooked table. The eyes
Of the dead calf are finally shut. The dating
Couples are dated. The pendulum is still
And time runs down like water from the hill.

4

Returning to the green mare. She is grinning
At the wild commotion. All those words and colours
Merely confirm her own view of aesthetics:
No artist ever paints quite what he sees.
No artist ever tries to paint his dreams.
An artist only paints what he believes in.
And she is winking, full of self-belief
And green intestines, though she knows the town
Is changing irredeemably behind her.
She tells the cows: your freedom is exciting.
She tells the cows: prepare for government.

BUDAPEST POSTCARDS:

REBUILDING THE CATHEDRALS

Everything has turned to foam.
Look, the tower rises and disintegrates
into thrusts and counterthrusts of lace,
a jostling of fine bones.

The hill has fallen into the river.
What remains rears up and stiffens.
The roofs are a shower of epaulettes,
ridiculous uniforms.

Nothing is as it seems – everything changes.
Foam tumbles and snaps like bone;
the lace inclines to rain;
the rain breaks up the fountain; time stands still.

BALLOON ADRIFT, CITY PARK

The children drift like feathers
   about the closing park.
The birds themselves are returning to the ark
   of the trees. A night
of softness is promised, an undisguised delight
   of late spring weather.

One balloon drifts upwards
   and slowly diminishes,
swaying slightly with tiny flourishes
   of its rabbit ears.
It takes some time before it disappears
   and quietly explodes.

ATTENDANTS OF THE METRO MUSEUM

How carefully the old custodians
of national treasures polish their black shoes
   and play up to their audience
of children, tourists, television crews.

It's something – even this – at such an age,
to trim your nails, refrain from picking your nose,
   to swot up an official page
of gangling facts in unremarkable prose.

They have a faint religious glow, like mystics
of some ancient orthodoxy playing host
   to a congregation of statistics,
attendant angels on a holy ghost

who is longing to embrace them finally.
They are proud to be the servants of the state,
   part of that great family
of dead who sit round patiently and wait.

IN THE PUPPET THEATRE

I never liked the way the usherettes
drew the curtain. We sat in a cigar box
        watching wooden faces
performing before coloured blocks
that made up into complicated sets
        of houses, palaces,

their legends hammered to a public shape
and rigged out with a song or two. We sat
        and watched and applauded,
singing and laughing at all of that,
but feeling still uneasy about the drape
        as if something sordid

were being acted out by woodentops,
so stiff and masklike – a whole mode of being –
        that we could not summon
arguments against it. And the puppets, seeing
        in this nothing uncommon,
rattled through their lines and moved the props.

TENEMENT

The face has its own architecture. See
   the tenants shift behind
half open curtains. It is like those maps
phrenologists would draw last century,
as if each mind contained a hundred minds,
so many minds the building should collapse
     under the weight
but somehow holds together, stands up straight.

How can one keep an eye on all these people,
   these obsessive couples
in their fury of daily living? I can hear
but cannot make out every syllable.
They speak in tiny streams of coloured bubbles
which issue from their mouths and disappear
    in the blue sky
which swallows them. And soon the mouths are dry.

THE CHILD I NEVER WAS

The child I never was could show you bones
that are pure England. All his metaphors
are drawn from water. His ears admit the sea
even to locked rooms with massive doors.

Look, let me make him for you: comb his hair
with venus comb, a wicked drupe for mouth,
twin abalones for ears, sharp auger teeth,
an open scalloped lung, a nautilus
for codpiece, cowrie knuckles, nacreous.
Let him shiver for you in the air.

The English schoolboy cannot understand
a country that is set in seas of land.

The child I never was makes poetry
of memories of landscape haunted by sea.
He stands in an attic and shows you his collection
of huge shells, and with an air of introspection
cracks his knuckle bones.

THE DUMMIES

The enormous matrons lose their heads –
a childish cancellation: you are dead.
The matron's belly and bust remain however,
admonitory presences or tailor's dummies
broadening with years to strapping ghosts.

Mothers, aunts, fat women in the street
parade their wardrobes, their corsets of caged wire.
The clothes that die in childhood are the first death,
faces merely fade, all limbs are guesses,
the hands are gloved and pocketed.

The traffic is a rattling in the street,
an opening of purses, a raised hat.
The wire cages sing with pointed birds
and curiosity. You laugh with careful teeth
and recognise the angels by their clothes.

A SMALL GIRL SWINGING

When first they pushed me
  I was very scared.
My tummy jiggled. I was
  Unprepared.

The second time was higher
  And my ears
Were cold with whisperings
  Of tiny fears.

The third time up was HIGH,
  My teeth on edge.
My heart leapt off the bedroom
  Windowledge.

The fourth time, Oh, the fourth time
  It was mad.
My skirt flew off the world
  And I was glad.

No one's pushing now,
  My ears are ringing.
Who'll see across the park
  A small girl swinging?

Who'll hear across the park
  Her mother calling,
And everywhere her shadows
  Rising, falling?

MEETING, 1944

(L.S. and M.S.)

I opened the front door and stood
lost in admiration of
a girl holding a paper box,
and that is how I fell in love.

I've come, she said, *to bring you this,*
some work from the photographer –
or rather it's for a Miss D . . .
Would you pass it on to her?

She's my sister, but she's out.
You must wait for her inside.
I'm expecting her right now.
Come in. I held the front door wide.

We talked a little of the war,
of what I did and what she earned;
a few minutes it was, no more,
before my sister had returned.

You're going? Well, I'm off out too.
And so we rose from our two chairs.
I'll be back shortly, Lily dear.
Shall I see you down the stairs?

That's all there is. We met again
until they took the Jews away.
I won't be long. I'll see you soon.
Write often. What else could we say?

I think they were such simple times
we died among simplicities,
and all that chaos seemed to prove
was what a simple world it is

that lets in someone at the door
and sees a pair of lives go down
high hollow stairs into the rain
that's falling gently on the town.

CHANGING NAMES

I started off with one name, which got lost,
and so I had to steal another one –
it was like changing places with a ghost.
I thought I'd keep it for a year at most,
Whatever you do once, the thing stays done.

I started with a lousy character
but bravery came with the change of face,
and that's the side of me that I prefer
(my girlfriend too says it appeals to her,
but she was hot for me in any case).

I started with an undeveloped member
which wouldn't stand – or it was hard to tell,
but now it's one a girl likes to remember
along with Roman Candles in November,
with some left over for next year as well.

I started somewhere in the middle class
(we might have had a cook, perhaps a maid)
but poverty is far more glamorous,
and what I lost in cash I've gained in brass.
The past is only there to be mislaid.

When fighting broke out I was pretty tough
(I can be quite a bastard when I like)
and once I shot a soldier, true enough –
a single bullet saw the bugger off.
I left him lying by his motor-bike.

Although I'm different, yet I'm much the same,
and that is what, I think, experience shows.
You change your shirt but cannot change the game.
As somebody once said, What's in a name?
A rose is just a rose is just a rose.

I've seen so many ghosts over the years
to have become one now is no surprise –
I feel the filmy gown as close as tears,
but nothing is as plain as it appears.
You kick the world and it dissolves, like lies.

BOYS WATCHING AN AEROPLANE DROP LEAFLETS

An incident from 1948

Where does it come from, this blown paper
littering the city squares,
these feathers left by birds on grass,
those clouds drifting unawares
and breaking softly against glass?

Appearing suddenly, the aeroplane
rocks the bay. All those waves.
She sets trees shaking and boats
bobbing, narrowly shaves
the hill, avoiding its throat,

But not its children, playing at war,
who do not hear the oracle
but see the falling of white leaves
as something of a miracle –
the liberation of handkerchiefs.

CULTURAL DIRECTIVES

As Michelangelo, the great Italian composer,
once remarked: Artists have responsibilities.
Hearing music is like contracting a disease,
a beautiful infection. It brings closer
the point of no return. One must be strong.
There's no such creature as a harmless song.

Painting too, as the English artist Shakespeare
pointed out, can be debilitating
unless you aspire beyond paint to real things.
A painting freezes movement. The eye, like the ear,
is a channel of impotence. Mere airs and graces
often induce an unproductive stasis.

And as for words, I only need quote Mozart,
the Swiss poet: They're tainted by unreason.
Language is discourse, words slippery. To seize one
we must lay traps, as for mice. The throat's part
of the respiratory tract, and you may clip
a speech, like air, by tightening your grip.

Too many of you are wasting your time and ours
with gewgaws, bric-à-brac and frolicking.
It's time to give you all a rollocking.
We're not impressed, I fear, by your endeavours.
The role of the past is to prepare the future
and your task is to welcome it with Culture.

AFTER ATTILA

(A version after Attila József)

The storm arrives, a froth of black,
A dark and sullen lumbering;
Lightning snickers, cuts a track
Of light across the slumbering
Landscape, like a shot of pain
Under the scalp, and then again,
A velvet shimmering and rumbling
Sets the jasmin quietly trembling.

See, apple-blossom – the twig is snapped –
Her petals, those poor butterfly-wings,
Attempt to fly, the foolish things.

Down the gentle slope the trapped
Mobs of wild grass bend and sway
Fearing the dark has come to stay.

Their shuddering, however frail,
Is good to teach their little ones
To bear the terror of the gale;
Learn then, my dear, when trouble comes
To sing your terror soft and low
So that the very grass may know
Your voice, and think that, as you pass,
You yourself are only grass.

THE BIRDS COMPLAIN

Tiny birds hatch tiny strategies
to lead men from their nests
hidden in low shrubs or wayside hedges;
they scream or tut, expose a barrel chest
or flash a wing.
We cannot guess their scale of suffering.

A brave performance, playing on the nerves,
instinctive as despair,
will get all the applause that it deserves.
Though much of it's mere sawing of the air
yet we are gripped
by truth, the very crudeness of the script.

CRUSE

Holding this cruse of bone, the human head,
    how brittle
the world appears. The strange occipital
    tenderness
of couples curled together in a bed
    is all they possess,

something to be packed away in cases
    of stoneware,
Meissen crockery, addressed to nowhere.
    They retain
their proper outward form, their public faces
    like old porcelain.

Such frailty (when the head's a passive thing,
    defenceless
without aid of arms) is almost senseless
    and unfair.
How lovely is the bone beneath the swing
    and softness of hair.

GLASS

He kept on dropping things. While I was there
He dropped two glasses, one bottle, tripped over my bag.
Each time a nervous smile, a slight sag
Of the shoulders, a vague look into the wild air,
Then out would come the broom. Behind the bar
    The glasses trembled,
    The glasses shimmered,
    The place resembled
A jeweller's window, the muscular
And nervous delicacy of the timid.

To be so clumsy was embarrassing.
He looked down frequently for crumbs of glass
And went on serving in that curious
Unsteady way of his, a wretched thing,
Enormous eared and fisted. Behind the bar
    The glasses trembled
    And dissembled
    In the honey-
Coloured light, displaying the muscular
And nervous delicacy of money.

MEETINGS

Drowned men return, the travellers come home,
All is forgiven in that breathless cry.
The statue weeps secure beneath her dome,
Delightedly she wipes her stony eye.

It is the end of literature to meet
With what was offered once and then withdrawn,
To make up stories and to give the sweet
Illusion that we're only as alone

As we would wish. I wish now we had kissed
Before you left me, but it is too late.
I cannot find your ear or lip or breast.
I'm going back to books. The rest can wait.

FROM THE HUNGARIAN

FORCED MARCH

Miklós Radnóti (1945)

He's foolish who, once down, resumes his weary beat,
A moving mass of cramps on restless human feet,
Who rises from the ground as if on borrowed wings,
Untempted by the mire to which he dare not cling,
Who, when you ask him why, flings back at you a word
Of how the thought of love makes dying less absurd.
Poor deluded fool, the man's a simpleton,
About his home by now only the scorched winds run,
His broken walls lie flat, his orchard yields no fruit,
His familiar nights go clad in terror's rumpled suit.
Oh could I but believe that such dreams had a base
Other than in my heart, some native resting place;
If only once again I heard the quiet hum
Of bees on the verandah, the jar of orchard plums
Cooling with late summer, the gardens half asleep,
Voluptuous fruit lolling on branches dipping deep,
And she before the hedgerow stood with sunbleached hair,
The lazy morning scrawling vague shadows on the air . . .
Why not? The moon is full, her circle is complete.
Don't leave me, friend, shout out, and see! I'm on my feet!

ARS POETICA

Ottó Orbán (1981)

'My art, my delectation . . .'?
   My art, my arse!
This stubborn growth, this irritation,
   This scratching place.

Yes, in my adolescence
   Art was a live
Creature – now it's merely the means
   By which I live.

So far, so good. Comme ci,
   Comme ça – but me,
I've little left to burn. You'll see
   A spark of fury,

A world stiffened by spite,
   Some frozen boughs
Observed down telescopic sights
   Through half-shut eyes.

But 'Art, my delectation . . .'?
   Of course, it's true.
Something beyond mere passion
   Burns briefly through

The world of all-there-is,
   Past form, past lust –
The shot deer pants and scurries,
   Then hits the dust.

PIETIES FOR SEPTEMBER

Dezsö Kosztolányi (1935)

September morning, enfold me in your glory,
don't leave me, don't desert me, September light,
now, when you blaze out, inflammatory,
leaping, tranced and conjured as my sight;
lift me to you, higher, one more time
to death on superannuated ruins,
help me, September, let me cling and climb
to you my brother, burning and renewing.
I've never bowed to those pale imitations
that other people scrape and mumble to,
I know what cold is coming. It's to you
I turn, true heathen, for illumination.
We belong together; see, my god,
I stand before you with my own acclaim,
fresh images still quickening my blood,
still vigorous (the girls will not complain).
I have no wish to drink the cellar dry
or glut myself on high cuisinery.
I'd sooner raid that storehouse of belief
eternity has hoarded and defy
the void with never-ending signs of life.
You bring on the ripe clusters of the vine,
my patron and protector, hand of fate;
bring me on too, I tremble on your line,
but look, my spirit and my spine are straight.
My arm still has the power to command;
another draught, another, ever fill
and ever gild, immeasurable hand;
my head's unbowed, no autumn shows there still.

The melon yields her ripeness; white as milk
her baby teeth are sparkling in the gum;
exhausted wasps find shelter in the silk-
soft garages of flowers in full bloom;
the grapes are almost splitting with their sweetness;
struck dumb with joy, the mouth is rendered speechless.

To what enchanted country have we come?
The time wings by. To satisfy our hunger
an unabated banqueting goes on
with lengthy lunches, suppers even longer.
My sister's in the garden gathering flowers,
the bowl she washes in each dawn is golden
and when she walks the woods at a late hour
the night stars sprinkle her with golden pollen.

It's exactly as it was in childhood,
the adults talking incomprehensibly
among themselves, each random noise a rude
interruption, the night wind's sobbing breath
exacerbated by some dreadful tree
whose dark boughs hint of winter, mud and death.

And yet the afternoon is stranger still,
shadows prepare the sunlight's funeral,
an ancient country piano begins to trill
the Pathétique (another dying fall),
or soul-sick Schumann, desolate and sweet,
stumbling over the keyboard, dumb with grief,
a melancholy yielding no relief
but schizophrenic laughter through clenched teeth.

The earth has never been so richly tinged
with madness and enchantment, the trees prattle,
the sky drops loops of crazy colour, fringed
with bright vermilion flaming into purple,
the dusk blows kisses to the mist and sinks
with her in one enormous wave of pink.
Tell me, if you can, what place this is,
what lost domain of childhood fantasies?

But ugly things delight us here no less,
despair and pain, the beggar's wretchedness,
look, this tiny church along the way,
how quietly it blazes at midday,
a peasant girl is mouthing to the Lord,
the blind rotate their eyeballs heavenward
as if under hypnosis, vacuous,
a deaf man strains to catch God's own clear voice.
At night your eye can hardly pierce the murk
of a small shop – the cobbler is at work
with one dim light to guide his operations
as in some pious book of illustrations.

But now the rain is black, one gushing stream,
and something glimmers in the fetid air
mysteriously, a parallelogram
gold through dark rain, a window's magic square.
Outside, the storm, a dull exhausted moaning,
inside, electric light, an autumn cleaning;
prepare for winter, the long promised season.
So tall a sky, such wonder beyond reason.

Why are the stars so huge today, of all days?
Each afternoon the kitchen is ablaze
with crockery, delightful to the senses.
What is one to do with confidences
of this nature? Whose epiphanies
are these? Who buffs the hills and scours the sky?
What pantheistic store of memories
invites me to relive the centuries?
Orion's helmet – is it sparkling still?
Why are all things laundered in this thick
celestial vapour? Who's responsible?
Why stare, enchantress, when it's only magic?

Sweet flame of being, may your fire be drawn
however aimlessly, through dusk and dawn,
arrest the clock and calendar, destroy
this rotting intellectual granary,
and raise my flag of youth, in attitudes
of grace, above the festive altitudes.